CHRISTIANITY

R. O. Hughes

Director of Education, Diocese of Salisbury

SERIES EDITOR: CLIVE ERRICKER

Lecturer in Arts Education
University of Warwick

Longman

About the Themes in Religion series

This series of books offers a lively and accessible introduction to the six main world religions for students taking GCSE Religious Studies. The books can be used separately to study one religious tradition, or they can be used together, to investigate one theme across the traditions, such as beliefs, worship, pilgrimage or values. The section on values shows how each religion reacts to everyday life and the modern world. The spreads offer class activities and assignments that relate to coursework requirements and encourage further research, and each book provides a glossary of important terms and a reading list.

Each spread is self-contained and presents an important aspect of each religion. Through carefully chosen photographs, clear text and relevant quotations from scriptures and believers, students will learn about each religion and the living impact it has for believers today. The wide variety of assignments help pupils to evaluate what they have read, suggest activities to further their understanding, and raise issues for them to reflect on.

We hope that these books will provide students of all abilities with a stimulating introduction to these religions, and that the enjoyment of using them matches that of producing them.

Clive Erricker

About Christianity

There are hundreds of millions of people in every part of the world, speaking almost every language in it, who have one thing in common: they describe themselves as Christians, as followers of Jesus Christ. What that means for their lives, their beliefs and their behaviour varies enormously, but all accept that Jesus is the clue to life's meaning. Like John's Gospel they believe he is 'the way, the truth and the life'. What does it mean to think like this? What difference does it make to a person's life? This book is like a series of snapshots from a family photograph album – giving a glimpse of what it means for different groups and individuals to call themselves 'Christian'.

These pictures of Christian life provide students with a firm basis from which to explore further, encouraging them to see that Christianity is not simply a subject in an examination syllabus but is about real people trying to make sense of their lives and to express the truths they believe.

R. O. Hughes

CONTENTS

THE CHRISTIAN LIFE

● Choose one of the pictures and tell a partner what you think is happening – as if you were present. Tell them what you see around you. Describe how you feel about what is happening. Say whether you understand what is happening. Get your partner to do the same for one of the other pictures. Then together write down *one* reason why you think what is happening in each event is taking place in a church.

A life's work

A parish **priest** talks about sharing in these special events:

'I've spent most of my life in poor parishes in big cities; terrible conditions – slum homes, bad health, people with no jobs, very little hope of getting one. I've been attacked in the streets and insulted and shouted at more times than I can remember. I was talking about all this in a school in the country and most of the class looked at me as if I was mad. Eventually one of them interrupted. "Why do you do it? Why do you keep on doing it?" For a moment I couldn't answer. Why did I go on year after year? Then I said, "I get one privilege most people don't get. I am allowed to share in the big moments of people's lives. If most people draw a graph of their lives there are only a few really big events, and I share them with people in my parish. I marry them and baptise their children. I prepare them for first Communion and confirmation. In some places I've stayed long enough to marry the children I baptised. I visit them when they are sick, help their parents and grandparents and prepare them for death, take their funerals and help them get over their sadness. If they want me, I'm around for the good and the bad – helping them to share with other Christians and to understand what God wants for them."'

ASSIGNMENTS

● Sometimes people get married or have their baby baptised in a church to please their family even though they never go to church themselves. Discuss in your group how many would be prepared to do the same. Write up their arguments for and against.

● With two partners imagine a meeting between a priest or minister and a couple who wanted their baby baptised but didn't think the promises involved very important and hadn't been to church since they were children. Write up a conversation they might have and role play your ideas for the rest of the group.

KEY WORDS

priest

BAPTISM

In the beginning

The parents and godparents with the baby all stood round this big bowl near the main door. The man in charge wore a long dress and said lots of words, while the other people kept their eyes shut. He asked the people to make promises. Then the man took the baby in his arms and, dipping his finger in the water, made a sign on the baby's forehead, just as if you were drawing on a window. He asked the baby's names and the mother said 'Claire Louise' but didn't give the surname. The man poured a small amount of water three times over the baby's head. The baby cried but the man wiped the water away and then handed the baby back to her mother. Lastly he said more words and gave me a lighted candle to hold.

● This is a child's eye view of infant baptism. How much of what he saw can you explain? Use the picture on the previous page to help you.

Christians believe that in **baptism** the baby
a) becomes a member of the Christian family
b) receives God's Holy Spirit into their life
c) receives the promise of God's forgiveness and strength.

A different viewpoint

The woman in the picture is also being baptised. What are the two main differences between this and the first baptism?

'I was very nervous but I knew this was what I wanted to do. As a Baptist, I had always been taught that I should make the Christian promises for myself as an adult. Going right down under the water was scary but I knew it was meant to show I had died to my old life and been born to a new one. I had publicly committed myself to be a follower of Jesus, and God would give me his spirit of love and power to strengthen me.'

● Read the quotation and look at the picture. How do they help you explain the differences between this and infant baptism? Share your ideas with a partner.

Other Christians as well as **Baptists** believe in adult baptism by total immersion in water. In place of infant baptism they often have a special service of infant dedication – to thank God for the new baby and to pray that they will be brought up in a loving and Christian home.

● How and why was Jesus baptised? Look up Matthew 3:13–17. What do you think actually happened?

ASSIGNMENTS

● With a partner make up your own infant baptism service. You can use ideas from the baptism service but add any of your own ideas as well. Remember to say whether you would have any music or singing, any special symbols or special presents.

● Children baptised as babies naturally say: 'I can't remember anything about it.' Using the information you have got and the baptism service from one of the prayer books listed on page 64, provide four or five cartoon pictures with captions to explain to a seven-year-old what happened at their baptism and what it meant.

KEY WORDS

baptism   Baptist

Baptism by total immersion

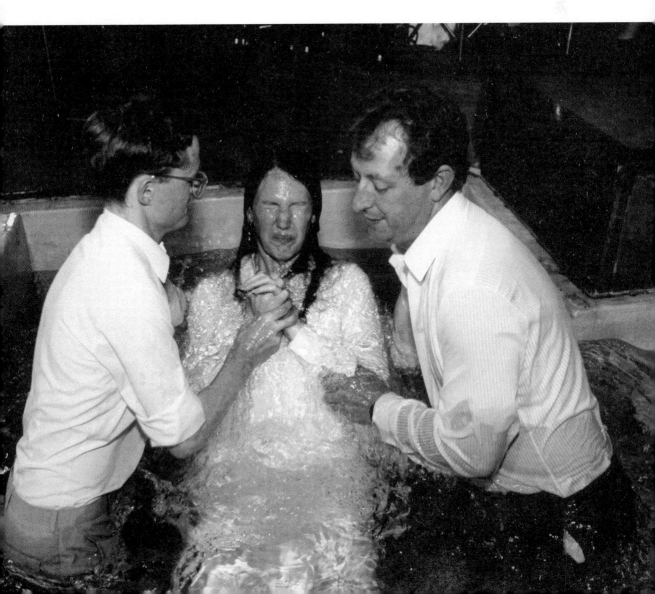

TAKING RESPONSIBILITY

● Think back to when you were 11 years old. Make a list of some of the things you can do now which you weren't allowed to do when you were that age. Does getting older seem to involve more freedom, or more responsibility? Why are you allowed to do more than you used to be? What has changed?

When a baby is baptised the parents and godparents take responsibility for bringing the child up properly within the Christian family. But eventually the person has to decide whether to take this responsibility

for themselves. In the Anglican and Roman Catholic Churches this is called **confirmation**. Samantha describes what happened to her:

'I wanted to be confirmed like my friends, so that I was more a part of the Church, and become like the adult members. I wanted to receive the Holy Communion and feel a closer link with God.

In the preparation the rector talked about what it meant to be confirmed and what was involved in it. We talked about the service and the rector explained the service book's deeper meaning, picking out quotes like "I turn to Christ" and explaining them. We saw the film slides on the Life and Death, the Teaching of Jesus, Baptism and the Church. Before the confirmation service we had a rehearsal in the church so that we knew exactly what to do.

Finally my confirmation day came and at 7.00 p.m. I was in the church putting my white veil on. Before I was confirmed I was baptised; after my baptism I returned to my seat. Then with the other girls who were to be confirmed we went forward to receive the blessing from the Bishop of Crediton who confirmed us. Next we went to receive our first Communion. Now that I am confirmed I feel I belong to the Church. I feel a much closer link to God, and the Sunday service now has a deeper meaning for me.'

● Samantha gives a lot of reasons why her confirmation was important. Make a list of what you think are the three main reasons. Look carefully at the picture. What do you think the girl in the photo might be thinking at this moment? What might she be feeling? What question would you most like to ask her about this experience?

Different practices

In the Church of England most young people don't share the **Communion** – receiving the bread and wine – until they are confirmed. In the Roman Catholic Church children receive their first Communion at seven and are confirmed later. First Communion is a very special day. In the Orthodox Churches a baby is confirmed straight after baptism. The child becomes a full member and able to receive Holy Communion in one special service of baptism and confirmation together.

ASSIGNMENTS

● Design a card for someone's confirmation *or* first Communion *or* adult baptism. Include a picture of what happens in the ceremony and a sentence of congratulation for the person receiving the card. Explain your card to a partner, showing you understand what the ceremony is all about.

● A friend says they are only going to be confirmed to please their parents. Discuss this view in groups and record the views and arguments for and against it, including your own opinion on this.

KEY WORDS

confirmation   Communion

MARRIAGE

● You have just come back from the wedding shown in the picture. You now have to write a letter or telephone a friend describing what happened because they couldn't go. Use the picture to work out what you are going to say. Add any knowledge of your own from your experience of weddings. Share your ideas with the group, then write your letter or act out what you would say on the telephone.

Most Christians want to have God's blessing on their new relationship and to make their vows in a church or chapel.

'Most people said I would be in such a daze I wouldn't remember anything that happened. But I do remember walking down the aisle on my dad's arm and seeing Martin look at me when I put my veil up. We were both nervous at making the promises and saying the vows but the vicar must have done hundreds of weddings. Martin couldn't get the ring on my finger and I started to put his ring on the wrong hand. But when Mr Phillips joined our hands together and then pronounced us man and wife, giving us God's blessing, I felt so happy. Coming back down the aisle together there were so many people I knew – all smiling – but it was my mum's face I'll never forget – all happy and sad at the same time.'

● Imagine you are a Christian planning to have a religious wedding. Make a list of questions you want to ask a priest or minister. Invite a minister to the class to answer your group's questions.

● With a partner look up the marriage promises in one of the prayer books listed at the end of this book.
a) Divide the promises into those you would find easy to make or keep, and those you would find difficult.
b) Discuss how you think Christians believe God helps them to keep the promises.
c) If the promises were rewritten 'To love (as long as I still like you) and to cherish (while I still enjoy your company) till death us do part (or until I get bored with you)' would these be more realistic? Why couldn't most Christians accept them? Share your ideas with your partner.

Symbols

A Christian marriage service is full of symbols and symbolic actions. You will find some in the picture and in the quotation above. In an Orthodox marriage service there are others: lighted candles, crowns or garlands, a goblet of wine.

ASSIGNMENTS

● Make a list of the symbols you can find in the photo and the quotation. Add the Orthodox symbols to your list. Use the books listed on page 64 to find out what they represent. Draw the symbols and write a short explanation in your own words.

● Imagine you have to produce a short film or slide sequence to explain what happens in a Christian marriage service to someone who has never been inside a church. Decide on three or four pictures or shots to illustrate the main points of the service and write a commentary to go with them. Share your suggestions in small groups and decide how well the pictures would help the person to understand the service.

AN END AND A BEGINNING

People everywhere try to make sense of death. Churchyards are full of inscriptions that show the sadness of death and the hope that it isn't the end. Sometimes there is humour as well. This is a genuine old inscription:

Here lies Solomon Peas
Under the trees and sod.
But Peas is not here –
Only the pod.
Peas shelled out and is gone to God.

● What is the inscription trying to say about death?

A Christian talks about attending the funeral of her husband:

'Most of the time I felt completely stunned. It could not be happening to me. It did not seem real sitting in a funeral car and following the coffin into the crematorium. Only last week we came back from holiday. When I was not crying I felt so angry with the world – with God for letting it happen to Geoff.

Part of me didn't want to listen to the words of the minister. Didn't want any comfort. But somehow the words kept getting through – like a radio signal coming and going. "Though he were dead yet shall he live." "In my Father's house are many mansions . . . ." "Let not your heart be troubled." And as we sang Geoff's favourite hymn it suddenly struck me. God wouldn't let him go. *We* had to let him go. But all that was precious and special about Geoff – his daft sense of humour and his kindness – somehow God wouldn't just let that waste to nothing. There had to be more than that. I don't know what I was supposed to think. I didn't hear a lot of what the minister said. But when he said the last prayer and the coffin began to disappear behind the curtain, it made some sort of sense to me. "Therefore commit his body . . . in the sure and certain hope." Sometimes only those words kept me going through the black patches and dark times until I began to see the light again.'

● Look at the picture and read the quotation carefully. Try to describe the different emotions the woman in the passage is feeling. Is this how you would expect someone to feel in this situation? What do you think is the 'sure and certain hope' which seems to help her?

ASSIGNMENTS

● Look at the funeral service in one of the prayer books listed on page 64. Christians often have two special readings from the Bible at a funeral service – John 14:1–6 and Psalm 23. Read them and put what they are saying into your own words. Add a piece explaining why you think many Christians find them helpful.

● You have to write a letter to a friend, one of whose close relatives has died. What would you say? How would you try to help them? How would your letter be different if you were a Christian? Do you think it helps people if they believe in life after death? Think about these things then write your letter as if you were a Christian.

VICTORY

From darkness to light

● Your closest friend comes to you in complete despair. Something has happened to make life utterly black and unbearable for them. What could you share from your own experience to show them that the darkness and misery won't last for ever? Share your ideas with a partner.

Charismatic Christians at worship

Christian belief begins with an amazing discovery made by the friends of Jesus. He was put to death on a cross on the first Good Friday, but this wasn't the end of the story. Their black despair was transformed by the events of the first Easter Day. Read the last chapter of Matthew's Gospel and the modern version of events opposite. The writer imagines Mary Magdalen, one of Jesus' followers, being questioned in a court room.

'You say he was in control. You mean before he died?'

'Even before he died. You know what his name means, don't you? Jesus – Joshua – the Conqueror. That's the only way to describe him. He was a man who had won.'

'But he didn't win. At the end, he was defeated.'

She shook her head, the bright flame of her hair swinging. 'No. That's what we thought. Last Friday afternoon that's the way it looked even to us. But now, everything's changed.'

'Since yesterday morning?'

'Yes.'

'I wonder if you could tell us what happened then, Miss Magdala? At the tomb, I mean.'

'He broke out. Nothing they could do could hold him.' She laughed, spreading her hands in a gesture of excitement. 'They sealed up the tomb, you know, and mounted a guard. It was ridiculous. Pathetic. Like tying up a sleeping lion with cotton thread. When he wakened he just snapped the thread and strode out.'

Mary is describing the **Resurrection**.

● Reread the passage and look at the picture. Then describe what you think Christians mean by the Resurrection.

It's dark now –
And I'm flying low,
Cold.

But deep within me
I remember
A darkness like this
That came before.
And I remember
That after that hard dark
That long dark –
Dawn broke.
And the sun rose
Again.
And that is what I must
Remember now.

● Why is the idea of resurrection and new life important to Christians? Does this poem give you some ideas?

St Paul wrote to the Christians of his time: 'If Christ has not been raised from the dead, then we have nothing to preach and you have nothing to believe.'

● Read 1 Corinthians 15:13–19 in a Bible and decide with a partner what you think he meant.

ASSIGNMENTS

● The modern version above of Jesus' death and resurrection is based on the four accounts in the Gospels of what happened to Jesus. Read the account in Luke 24:13–35. Now imagine you were one of the two disciples who met Jesus on the road to Emmaus. Write a diary entry describing what happened to you. Include an explanation of why you didn't recognise Jesus at first and how you knew it was him later, and describe what you felt.

KEY WORDS

Resurrection

BELIEVING

I believe . . .

Some young people were asked what they believed. Here are some of their thoughts:

'I believe in God and his making of the world and life. Life is a wonderful thing. I do not believe in man from other planets. I like the wonderful nature. Animals and flowers, big and small. I like to be happy all the time. I do not fear death. I have many friends. I like sport.'
[10-year-old boy]

'I believe that there is life after death. When people die their body stops working and their soul ascends or stays on earth as a ghost. Then you come back into the world as another being, e.g. cat, dog or mouse.'
[13-year-old boy]

'I believe in making the most of life we can. Life is far too short to waste, just to sit around waiting for something to happen. Unknown to us, life is ticking away. Before long we will be raising our own family and not so long after that, knitting for our own family.'
[14-year-old girl]

● In a group try to write a 50-word statement beginning 'I believe a good school should . . .'. First discuss what makes a good school. Consider the various suggestions and then reduce them to 50 words. What difficulties did you have in getting everyone to agree? Was it difficult because you were discussing beliefs and values?

● Now write down some ideas of your own about some of your beliefs, beginning 'I believe . . .'. You might want to share this with a partner.

Christian beliefs

Christian statements of belief are called **creeds,** from the Latin word 'credo' meaning 'I believe'. They can be long or short.

● Look at the statement or creed in the picture. What do you think it means? How does it show the importance of the Resurrection to Christians? Why do you think it matters to the boy? Draw a quick pin-man sketch of yourself holding a banner. What message of belief would you want to put on it?

ASSIGNMENTS

● There is one prayer you would hear Christians using all over the world. It is another statement of what they believe, almost as short as your 50-word statement about the school. What is it? Try writing it down, or look it up in Matthew 6:9–13. Read it with a partner and decide what you think each line means.

● Most of the Christian prayer books listed on page 64 include two long creeds called the Apostles' Creed and the Nicene Creed. Find a copy of each and with a partner decide where they are the same and where they are different. Read from the Apostles' Creed first and then work out what extra ideas you find in the Nicene Creed. Then find two pieces of additional information from each of the creeds and try to explain them.

KEY WORDS

creed

PICTURES OF GOD

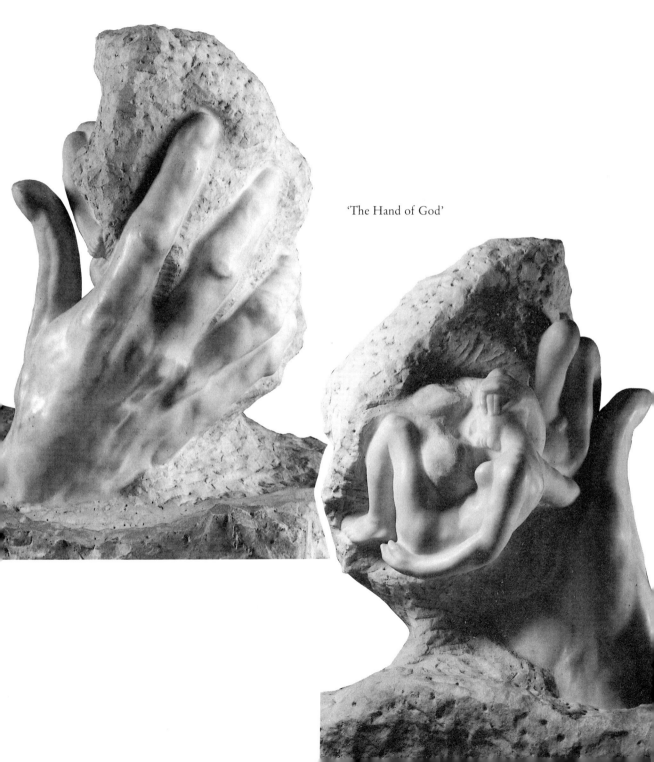

'The Hand of God'

This is what an eight-year-old boy wrote about his beliefs:

I believe in God because he's true.
I believe in books because we can read.
I believe in church because it is a holy place.
I believe in chairs because we can sit on them.
I believe in windows because we can look out.
I believe in mountains because we can climb them.

● With a partner think about what the boy is saying. Is he using the word 'believe' in the same way each time? If not, in what different ways is he using it? Does he believe in God for the same reason he believes in books or chairs? What is the difference?

Christians don't think they can describe God in the same way as you describe a chair or a mountain. The Bible is full of different pictures of God, beginning with the accounts of God as **Creator** in the book of Genesis.

A personal God

This is a poet's view (based on Genesis):

And God stepped out on space,
and looked around and said,
I'm lonely –
I'll make me a world.

And as far as the eye of God could see
Darkness covered everything.
Blacker than a hundred midnights
Down in a cypress swamp.

Then God smiled.
And the light broke,
and the darkness rolled up on one side,
and the light stood shining on the other.
And God said, that's good!

● What does the poet think about God? Do you think it makes it easier for Christians if they think about God in this personal way? Can you think of any problem in describing God in this way?

● Now look at the photographs which show an artist's view. The sculpture is by the French artist Rodin and is called 'The Hand of God'. What do you think Rodin is trying to say about God? Share your ideas.

ASSIGNMENTS

● The book of Psalms in the Old Testament is full of word pictures of God: God is King (Ps 93), Shepherd (Ps 23), Judge (Ps 82).
a) Look up these references. Draw a symbol for each word picture, then underneath write what you think the writer is saying about God.
b) Find at least three other descriptions for God in the Psalms.

● Why do you think it is very important to some Christians that the Bible also talks about God as a mother as well as a father? Write a short piece about this.

KEY WORDS

Creator

WHO IS JESUS?

One view of Jesus

When a new headteacher is appointed, everyone wants to know what they are like. Are they strict or easy-going, short-tempered or relaxed, likely to change everything or keep things as they are?

● On your own write a description of someone everyone in your group knows. Then compare what you have written. How much is the same? What is different? Why doesn't everyone agree? Can you explain the differences?

● Look at this modern picture of Jesus. Imagine you were one of the group shown watching him. Write a brief description of him. Compare and explain your ideas with the group as you did before.

God with us

A Christian wrote:

> For a long time I wanted to have nothing to do with God or Jesus. If they did exist, they had nothing to do with my life; they were no good to me. I needed someone who could understand about human life – about the good things, family fortunes, having a drink with friends, sharing a joke and a story. I wanted someone who knew about loneliness, and failure, and despair. And then one night I was on my own, and I watched one of those films about Jesus – because there was nothing else to watch. And I knew it was only actors but it started to dawn on me that Jesus did know about family and friends, he could understand about despair and failure.

> And if he had been God – as they'd always told me – God coming and sharing our human life, I might have to start taking God seriously.

● Read the extract carefully. What did the writer start to understand during the television film? Why did it make a difference to him/her?

What is God like?

The first Christians came to believe that Jesus was more than a very good man. In Jesus, God himself had come to share in human life. This is called the **Incarnation** (from the Latin 'in flesh'). Every part of his life, what he did and what he taught, showed them what God is like.

ASSIGNMENTS

● Here are six examples from Luke's account of what Jesus did:

Luke 5:12–13   Luke 7:1–9   Luke 8:22–5
Luke 9:12–17   Luke 14:1–6   Luke 15:4–7

a) Read three or more of them and using the two headings:

What Jesus Did   and   **What God is Like**

fill in what Jesus is doing and what it shows about God. For example in Luke 5:12–13 Jesus is healing the sick. The first Christians saw this as a sign that God wants health and wholeness for everyone.

b) Imagine you have to write a short talk about how a Christian should live. Write your talk, including some quotations from these passages.

KEY WORDS

Incarnation

WHY DID HE DIE?

Dying for others

Read this story from the Second World War:

When the German occupation of Paris took place, Mother Maria, a Russian Orthodox nun, summoned her chaplain and told him that she felt her particular duty was to give all the help she could to persecuted Jews. She knew this would mean imprisonment and probably death, and she gave him the option of leaving. He refused. For a month the convent was a haven for Jews. Women and children were hidden within its walls and hundreds got away. At the end of a month the Gestapo came. Mother Maria was arrested and sent to the concentration camp at Ravensbrück. Her chaplain was sent to Buchenwald where he died of starvation and overwork.

She was known even to the guards as 'that wonderful Russian nun' and it is doubtful whether they had any intention of killing her. She had been there two and a half years when a new block of buildings was erected at the camp, and the prisoners were told that these were to be hot baths. A day came when a few dozen prisoners from the women's quarters were lined up outside the buildings. One girl became hysterical. Mother Maria, who had not been selected, came up to her. 'Don't be frightened,' she said, 'look, I shall take your turn,' and, in line with the rest, she passed through the doors. It was Good Friday 1945.

This story was not made up. The events actually happened. They made such an impression on those who saw them that after the war they wrote them down to share with other people.

● Do you think Mother Maria was stupid to die when she didn't have to? Or do you think that bravery like this ought to be remembered? Discuss what you think in a small group.

● Now look at the sculpture for a few moments in silence. Write down any ideas or words that come into your head. What does the sculpture make you think of? Share your ideas with a partner.

The death of Jesus

There is no easy way to explain the meaning of Jesus' death for Christians. But some find the story of Mother Maria helps them to understand more about Jesus. In the face of great evil, the only way Mother Maria could save the terrified girl and help the frightened women was to take her

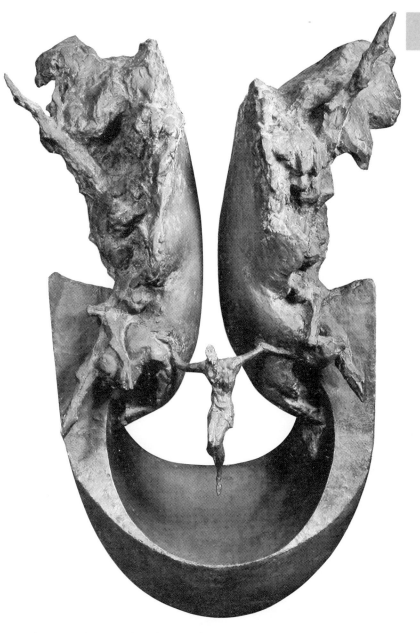

place and file into the gas chamber with the others.

For Christians, Jesus faced all the evil in the world. It threatened to cut human beings off from God. They couldn't do anything to help themselves because of their own sins. But Jesus stood in their place and willingly accepted all the evil thrown at him, and death on a cross. This is called the **Atonement** (at-one-ment).

ASSIGNMENTS

● Use the sculpture and the story of Mother Maria to help you explain the meaning of the word 'Atonement'. Then write another piece explaining why Christians believe Jesus defeated the power of evil and death, and gained the victory.

KEY WORDS

Atonement

WHAT IS WORSHIP?

Meeting together

● Make a note of any group you belong to, apart from your group at home or school. Underneath each group write a sentence describing its purpose.

Most people belong to groups because they share a common interest, they enjoy the company of other people and want to do things together. This is how two Christians explained why they meet with others for worship:

'We want to show our love for the Lord Jesus in our own way: clapping and dancing, singing with all our hearts, listening to the teaching, joining in with the speaker and the prayers. We don't mind anyone seeing how we feel. We've got a wonderful message and we want everyone to share it.'

'I go to the quiet early Communion service because it helps me feel closer to God. I know all the words and so I can think about what God wants me to do with my life. We try to have some silence so that people can have space for their prayers. I come away feeling better and stronger.'

● Look carefully at the two pictures of Christians meeting for worship and look again at the quotations opposite. Choose one person in each picture and look at them quietly for a few moments. Try to get inside what they are thinking and feeling. Then with a partner make a list of the reasons why you think Christians meet for worship.

Most Christian groups are influenced by the example of Jesus' first disciples. St Luke's account of the early Church in the Acts of the Apostles (2:42) gives a good summary of Christian worship:

> They [the first Christians] met constantly to hear the apostles teach, and to share the common life, to break bread, and to pray.

Did all four aspects of worship: teaching, sharing, Communion and prayer come up in your reasons why Christians worship together?

Remembering Jesus

For most Christians, the heart of their worship remembers Jesus' last meal with his disciples before his death, and what he said to them at that time. Christians call this meal the Last Supper, and in different ways they have included Jesus' words at this time in their services. You can find Jesus' words recorded in Luke's Gospel 22:17–19.

ASSIGNMENTS

● Read the account of the Last Supper in Luke's Gospel 22:7–20. Imagine you were one of the disciples sitting around the table at the meal. Using the understanding of the disciples' experience you have so far, write an explanation of what you thought Jesus meant and what it felt like to be at that meal.

● With a partner decide on six questions you would ask a Christian to find out about their worship. Using the books on page 64 discover how a member of the Church of England might answer your questions, or try them out on a Christian you know and write down their answers.

UNDERSTANDING COMMUNION

● With a partner make a list of the special things people wear or carry to remind them about someone they love. Why are they important?

These are more than photographs or letters, inexpensive crosses or medallions. A woman carries a holiday picture of her family. It reminds her of good times to remember and treasure. It reminds her that she is still loved and cared for by her family. When she is depressed or lonely the picture gives her strength and comfort.

Ways of remembering

Different groups of Christians understand Communion in different ways. But they all start with what St Paul wrote about the Last Supper (1 Corinthians 11):

> [23]For I received from the Lord what I also passed on to you: The Lord Jesus, on the night he was betrayed, took bread, [24]and when he had given thanks, he broke it and said, "This is my body, which is for you; do this in remembrance of me." [25]In the same way, after supper he took the cup, saying, "This cup is the new covenant in my blood; do this, whenever you drink it, in remembrance of me."

Most Christians also see the sharing of bread and wine as a **sacrament** – a visible way of showing that God is offering them his love. A **Methodist** describes their understanding of the Lord's Supper:

> 'When our minister breaks the loaf of bread and uses the words of Jesus at the Last Supper, it's as if that meal in the Upper Room was happening now and Jesus is telling all of us how much he loves us; enough to die for us. And we are all here together; all sharing the one loaf, all part of one community. The minister says: "The bread we break is a sharing in the body of Christ. Though we are many, we are one body because we all share in the one loaf." We are giving thanks for the life and death and resurrection of Jesus; because Jesus has shown us that nothing can separate us from the love of God. And every time I share in the Lord's Supper I come home determined to do my bit to spread that love in the world.'

Methodists describe the Lord's Supper in three ways: Memorial (remembering), Communion (sharing) and **Eucharist** (thanksgiving).

● Using the quotation and the picture, write a short explanation with a partner of each of these three descriptions.

ASSIGNMENTS

● Why do Christians usually talk about *Holy* Communion?
Are there other times when Christians use the word 'holy'?
Write a brief explanation of what you think the word means.

● Some groups of Christians believe that Jesus Christ is
present in the Holy Communion in a very special way. Use
the books on page 64 to discover how Roman Catholics
understand what happens. Share your findings then write a
dialogue between a Roman Catholic and a Methodist about
their different views.

KEY WORDS

sacrament   Methodist   Eucharist

Methodists share wine at their
Communion service

STYLES OF WORSHIP

● Try an experiment. Ask your partner:
  a) If football is played with the same-shaped ball and the same rules, why aren't all football games the same?
  b) If all music consists of the same notes and sounds, why doesn't it all sound the same?
  c) If all pictures are painted with similar brushes and paints, why are some pictures so very different from others?

People express themselves differently even though they are basically doing the same thing. Some of the differences in Christian worship are to do with temperament, some to do with different beliefs, some with different history.

Different needs

● Look at the two pictures. Both show Christians at worship. Make a list of the main differences between the styles of worship.

This is how a **Quaker** and then an **Orthodox** Christian describe their worship:

'We call our worship a "Meeting" and our Meeting Houses are usually very simple; they might have a text and some flowers but nothing else. A lot of the time we sit in silence waiting on God; sometimes different people want to share their prayer with us. You might find it rather dull but the Society of Friends has been worshipping like this for over three hundred years. We believe God's Inner Light can work in every individual and so we don't need special services or sacraments or priests.'

'For someone belonging to the Orthodox tradition like me, the worship, or **liturgy**, is the most important thing of all. When I tell my friends it often lasts over three hours they cannot believe me. But in our worship we remember all that Jesus did for us. The priest and deacon bring the Gospels in to the people to represent Jesus coming to earth. Then they bring the bread and wine to represent the entry into Jerusalem. The priest consecrates the bread and wine just like at the Last Supper and brings it out to the people. It's as if through the music and the prayer and the beauty we get a glimpse of heaven.'

● Using these two accounts and the pictures, try to explain some of the reasons for the differences between the two styles of worship.

Different beliefs

Worship expresses what people believe. If different Christian groups have different beliefs or a different history their worship will show this. Orthodox Christians make sharing the bread and wine central, while Friends (Quakers) don't believe this is necessary at all. **Protestant** Churches which split off from the Roman Catholic Church in the sixteenth century did not accept the Catholic ideas about the **Mass**, but put their main emphasis on reading and preaching from the Bible.

ASSIGNMENTS

● Write a brief introduction to worship in the Orthodox and Quaker traditions. Start by getting a partner or your teacher to look at the two pictures and then ask you questions about what you can see in each picture. Using the books on page 64, write out what you need to know to answer these questions.

KEY WORDS

Quaker   Orthodox   liturgy
Protestant   Mass

PLACES OF WORSHIP

● You live near the centre of a town. While there are still some people living in the area, most of the houses have been turned into shops and offices. The local church only gets a handful of people every Sunday and the church authorities have decided to close it and pull it down so that they can build shops and flats for elderly people in its place. The church building isn't very old or special but it has been a landmark in the area for over a hundred years. Your next-door neighbour wants your help to keep it open. With a partner, decide what arguments your neighbour might use to persuade you and what you would say in reply.

The two pictures show just how different Christian places of worship can be. Look at the detail of the pictures and decide which tradition each one represents – **Protestant** or **Roman Catholic**. Read the two quotations from people who worship in these traditions:

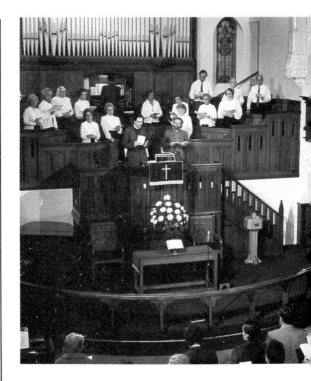

'Everywhere I look in our church there is something to point me to the beauty and mystery of our faith. There are stained-glass windows, statues, candles, pictures – all helping me to come close to God. The pointed windows and arches point up to heaven, the faint smell of incense reminds me of all the prayer that goes on, and the sanctuary light shows that the consecrated bread – the host – is kept, reserved, behind the altar. The whole rather dark and mysterious atmosphere of quiet and peace helps me to pray.'

'In our church we keep the decoration and trimmings down to the minimum. There are a few inscriptions round the walls, but everything is concentrated on the pulpit and the reading desk. My great-grandfather built this place and he didn't want anything to interfere with people hearing the word of God from the Bible and from the minister. In his day they only had Communion once every three months, and that's one of the reasons the Table for the Lord's Supper is so small.'

● Using the information in the pictures and the quotations, and what you already know about different types of church buildings, draw and label a simple diagram of what each building might look like. (It might help to know that one is rectangular and one is in the shape of a cross.) Then look at your drawings with a partner and decide:
a) what the focal point is in each of the buildings
b) whether the two buildings are decorated in the same way
c) what picture of Christianity and Christians you would get if you went into each of the buildings.

Remember, like styles of worship, places of worship tell us about a Christian group's special beliefs and history. Many Protestants disliked the candles, statues and pictures, the fine vestments and stained-glass used in Roman Catholic and many **Anglican** churches. They believed these could get in the way of thinking about God and listening to his message in the Bible. Their churches and chapels were therefore much plainer and simpler.

ASSIGNMENTS

● With a partner pick a local area you know well. Find out the different places of Christian worship in this area. Make a careful map and mark in the various places – providing a simple description of each place of worship. Check your suggestions with your teacher.

● Produce a simple leaflet for two different places of Christian worship describing what they are like, why they are like that and what happens in them. You might want to take your own photographs.

KEY WORDS

Protestant   Roman Catholic
Anglican

PRIVATE WORSHIP

Ways of praying

Christians describe prayer in many different ways. One Christian explained how he prayed:

'If I am honest, much of my prayer is taken up with petition – asking God for help and strength. I know it's no use asking for a new car or a win on the football pools but I do ask for patience when I am seeing a particularly difficult client and courage when the job is particularly difficult. And of course if I pray for help I've also got to include confession in my prayers, for all the times I've failed to show love and let my quick temper get the better of me. I suppose that's why I try to find time for meditation – letting my mind and body relax and focusing on one thought or idea so that I can be open to God. One thing that helps me is the Jesus prayer from the Orthodox Church. I found it in a book one day. I wrote it out and kept it:

"Sit down alone and in silence. Lower your head, shut your eyes, breathe out gently and imagine yourself looking into your own heart. Carry your mind, i.e. your thoughts, from your head to your heart. As you breathe out say 'Lord Jesus Christ, have mercy on me.' Say it moving your lips gently, or simply say it in your mind. Try to put all other thoughts aside. Be calm, be patient, and repeat the process very frequently."

I'm still not very good at it but it helps me to concentrate. And then finally of course there's thanksgiving – when I just want to thank God for something great that's happened.'

● With a partner work out three different sorts of prayer described in the quotation. Write a brief description of each one. What question(s) would you want to ask this Christian after reading his description of prayer?

Different Christians have different ways of trying to concentrate in their prayer. Roman Catholics and some other Christians use a **rosary** (as in the picture) – a collection of 165 beads – to help them concentrate. The beads are in groups and as each group passes through the fingers the person repeats the words of the Lord's Prayer, the Hail Mary and the Gloria. Many Christians have a **crucifix** (the figure of Christ on a cross) or a simple, plain cross in their homes.

Orthodox Christians often have pictures of saints or people from the Bible, called icons. An **icon** is a very special picture, painted with great love and care, which helps them to think about some qualities of God or Jesus. Similarly Roman Catholics often pray in front of images or statues of the saints or the Virgin Mary, and light candles in front of them. Catholics believe that the saints and the Virgin Mary can help their prayers and bring them closer to God.

● Why do you think many people find prayer difficult to understand? Make a list of possible reasons with a partner and then share them with the group.

ASSIGNMENTS

● Make a collection of pictures to show at least three different ways Christians are helped to pray. Use your pictures as the basis for a five-minute talk on 'Christian Prayer'.

KEY WORDS

rosary   crucifix   icon

THE BIBLE

A SPECIAL BOOK

The Gospel reading in an Anglican church

A book with authority

● Look at the picture. Describe what is happening. With a partner write down as many reasons as you can why the Bible is a special book for Christians.

Here are three Christians talking about the **Bible**. Each one is explaining why they respect the Bible so much:

> 'I read the Bible every night because it tells me how I ought to live. I think about Jesus' teaching and how I ought to behave as one of his followers.'
>
> 'There isn't any other book like the Bible. I wouldn't need anything else on my desert island. It tells you everything about God you need to know.'
>
> 'I get very upset when people treat the Bible like any other book, and leave it lying around to get tatty and torn. A book explaining the meaning of life is too special for that.'

Each person is also talking about something more than respect. For each of them the Bible has *authority*: it makes a difference to how they live.

● Try putting the three reasons why they think the Bible has authority into your own words.

This Christian adds one more essential word to any description of the Bible. Read the passage and then decide what is extra to the idea of respect and authority:

> 'I know when I read the Bible that this is God's way of telling me about himself and what he wants for us all. He inspired all the different writers: the story-tellers, the law men, the prophets and the poets. He opened their eyes. All the stories, and the laws, and the poems – they all show us what he is like. It's not just good or special or clever – somehow it comes from God himself.'

It is this idea of *inspiration* which makes the Bible so special. Some Christians think it makes the whole Bible literally true in every detail. Others believe the writers were inspired to use stories and poetry to talk about God.

ASSIGNMENTS

● A group of Christians was thinking about the Bible. They were given a number of sentences to complete:
a) When someone mentions the Bible I __
b) My earliest memory of the Bible is __
c) People I know seem to think the Bible is __
d) For me most of the Bible is __
e) My biggest difficulty with the Bible is __
Complete these sentences for yourself. Then imagine you are asked to talk to a class of children about why the Bible is special to Christians. Write your talk and/or speak it into a tape recorder. Think very carefully about what to include, and use a passage(s) from the Bible to help illustrate what you say. You may find completing the sentences again as if you were a Christian helps you do this task.

KEY WORDS

Bible

THE STORY OF THE BIBLE

A story told in many ways

It is very sad to go through the papers of a relative or friend after they have died. Often a desk drawer is crammed full of old papers, going back sixty or seventy years. There may be old love letters carefully tied up in a ribbon, old diaries, the details of clubs they once belonged to; masses of old bills, official letters from solicitors; old birthday cards with bits of poetry; sometimes even school reports and exercise books. There's the story of a life in all the old bits of paper – seen in lots of different ways but all telling the same story.

● What keepsakes and papers have you got which illustrate the story of your life? Make a list of three or four and think of a story connected with each one.

● Now make a list of six stories you know of from the Bible. You can see a Bible story in the photograph of the stained-glass window. Which story is being illustrated? What is it trying to show about God?

God and his people

There is one long-running story in the Bible – the relationship between God and his people. The relationship is described in many different ways.

Sometimes God appears as the character in a story. In Genesis 3:8 he walks in the garden at sunset looking for Adam and Eve.

Sometimes he is the central figure in the books of history. Elijah goes to confront God in 1 Kings 19 but finds he is not in the wind, the earthquake or the fire but in a 'still, small voice'.

Then again he's a law-giver setting out the terms of his agreement with the Jews in the books of the Law. In Exodus 20 the Ten Commandments are spelled out for the people.

At other times he is shown debating in an argument. The Book of Job ends with Job accepting that he will never win an argument with God (chapters 40–2).

Or he is a keeper, a guardian, a shepherd. Psalm 121 (Psalms is one of the books of poetry) describes God watching over his people at all times. 'The Lord will guard your going out and your coming in from this time forth for evermore.'

ASSIGNMENTS

● Imagine you are taking a Sunday School class. You can choose one of the five passages mentioned above to help the children understand how the Bible talks about God. Decide which one you would choose and write up how you would explore it with the children. Include practical activities like painting, drama and singing as well as talking.

Stories in glass

THE BIBLE IN PRIVATE PRAYER

If you stay in a hotel you will find details of the hotel services, tourist leaflets, emergency instructions, a telephone directory and ... a Bible, put there by an international group of Christian businessmen called the Gideons. They believe the Bible is not only for public worship but is also very important for private prayer and worship.

A Coptic Christian in Ethiopia reads his Bible

● Try and think of three reasons why the Christian businessmen might want every hotel room to have a Bible. Share and discuss these in your group. If you can, find out what the Gideons say about their work. (Look up their address in a phone book.) See if their reasons match yours.

The Bible at home

Millions of Christians believe that reading the Bible at home, often on a daily basis, helps them:

to understand more what God is like
to learn how they can best be disciples of Jesus
to find out how they should live their lives.

They read a passage every night, think quietly about what it means, and include it in their prayers. This is an English Christian describing her reading:

'I try to read the story slowly and quietly, pausing after each of the verses to let them sink in. Sometimes I imagine I was there in the hot sun listening to Jesus with all the others in the crowd. Last night I read a passage from St Matthew's Gospel: "Are not sparrows two a penny? Yet without your Father's leave not one of them can fall to the ground. As for you, even the hairs of your head have all been counted. So have no fear; you are worth more than any number of sparrows."

Sometimes I have to spend a long time trying to work out what the passage is telling me. I get confused and even a bit angry. How could God care for the sparrows when so many innocent people get killed every day? But I know it is not as simple as that, so often I just fix on one phrase and repeat the words to myself: "Have no fear ..." and sometimes it seems as if those words are being spoken just for me and my problems. And they help me with my prayers afterwards.'

Daily reading

This Christian might have been following a selection of passages from the Bible which some Churches, such as the Roman Catholic and Anglican Churches, set out for every day of the year. These lists are called a 'lectionary' and over a year- or two-year cycle they cover large parts of the Bible. She might also have been using one of the many Bible Reading notes which thousands of people use to help them understand more about the passage they are reading and what it could mean for them.

ASSIGNMENTS

● You may have been given a Gideon Bible at school. Your teacher will certainly be able to get an example of the sort of Bible the Gideons provide for hotels. All the Gideon Bibles have a section giving Bible references for people who are very unhappy or depressed. Read the references carefully to yourself and then write down why you think the words might, *or* might not, help someone who was really miserable. Rereading the explanation above by the Christian about how she reads a passage may help you with this.

THE BIBLE IN PUBLIC WORSHIP

Reading in public

● Have you ever had to make a speech or read in public? Many people have nightmares about forgetting their lines or saying the wrong thing. It takes courage to stand up in front of an audience. Share an experience of yours with a friend or with the group.

A famous television personality was asked if he would read at a Sunday church service sometime in the future. He agreed:

One Saturday a message arrived that he was 'on' at 11 o'clock next morning. Eamonn explained to the priest why he would have to refuse this time.

'The word of God,' he said, 'as far as I am concerned is something which is absolutely precious. It means an awful lot to me. I have made a lot of sacrifices during my life because of the convictions I have about the Gospel, and therefore I will not take the Gospel for granted.

You have asked me to come along tomorrow to go out and read something I never saw before. If I were doing a television programme I would spend a whole week planning and preparing it. I will not go out there and read in front of the people without putting a lot of preparation into it; without having it explained to me. I want to know what it is about. I want to pray about it.'

● Some people might say the broadcaster was making too much fuss. Could you explain what he was saying in your own words? Do you think he was right to refuse? How was he showing respect for the Bible?

Symbols of respect

Church services often have lots of clues showing the importance of the Bible, and especially the **Gospel** readings about Jesus and his teaching. In the Roman Catholic Church and some Anglican churches there is a Gospel procession. The Gospel book is carried by one of the servers, accompanied by a cross-bearer and candleholders, and read by one of the clergy with the people standing up and turning towards him. 'This is the Gospel of Christ,' he says at the end, and the people reply 'Thanks be to God.' (The photograph on page 34 shows the Gospel reading in an Anglican church.)

In many Orthodox Churches this is the climax of the first half of the service – the Ministry of the Word. The Book of Gospels, covered in precious metals and stones, is brought into the main area of the church for solemn reading. Then the book is kissed by the reader.

ASSIGNMENTS

● Look at the picture. Imagine you had to suggest a Bible passage for the preacher to talk about. Choose a text from one of the four Gospels and write a short piece explaining why you chose it. Write down also what you might say about the passage if you were the preacher.

● Christian hymns frequently emphasise the importance of the Bible. With a partner decide what this hymn is trying to say, and explain it as clearly as you can for someone who does not understand the Bible:

Thanks to God whose Word was written
　in the Bible's sacred page,
Record of the revelation
　showing God to every age.
　God has spoken
Praise him for his open Word.

KEY WORDS

Gospel

INTO ALL THE WORLD

Have you ever stood in a foreign airport or station and heard an important announcement in a language you couldn't understand? Have you ever looked at a road or information sign abroad and not been able to read what it said? Have you ever been into a restaurant and not been able to understand the foreign menu?

● With a partner or group, share any experience you have had like this. How did you feel? What did you do? How did you get help?

A Bible for everyone

Where does a new Christian who wants to understand the Bible in their own language get help? There are thought to be 16,500 new Christians each day in Africa – and all want to read the Bible in the language or dialect they speak. Here's a translator describing what he tries to do:

'You might think it is quite easy to translate the Bible because there are already so many different versions. But when you are translating for people in a country very different from that of Jesus', it produces some difficult problems. A hot country may have no word for snow, a flat country no word for mountain, a dry country no word for river.

You might think that every people would have an equivalent word for all the words in the Bible. But some words, like grace, or repentance, or forgiveness, don't exist in a particular language. The translator has to find a phrase which means the same, or as close to the original idea, as he or she can.

The Bible often uses word pictures to put across its meaning. In Revelation 3:20 (in the New Testament) Jesus is pictured standing at the door and knocking. But in parts of Africa, the only people who knock on a door are thieves trying to discover if there is anyone inside. A proper visitor stands outside, calls his name and waits to be invited in.

These are problems we try to solve by working with scholars who know the Bible well, and people who know the language and dialect well. But in some parts of the world there is no written form of the language at all, and that means a very big task.'

Christians in Papua
New Guinea listen
to a translation of the Bible
in their own language

ASSIGNMENTS

● Think about some of the translator's problems:
a) How else could he translate the phrase 'as white as snow'? (Matthew 28:3)
b) What phrase could he use instead of 'forgiveness'? (e.g. in Matthew 9:2)
c) How would you change the phrase from Revelation 'Behold I stand at the door and knock'?
d) Sometimes the translator is working for people who have no written language. Describe why this would be a major problem for the translator. Then suggest four things she or he would have to do to try to solve the problem.

● Write a letter to the translator telling him that he would do much better if he spent his time and money helping people improve their agriculture or health. Share your letters and then with a partner decide what you think the translator might write in his reply.

CELEBRATIONS

HIGH DAYS AND HOLY DAYS

● Imagine that all existing festivals and celebrations are banned. *You* must decide which six special days will be celebrated during the year. These might be religious festivals or be entirely non-religious. They might celebrate something national or international. They might be a special day for young people, or for sport or music or mothers. What would you choose? Draw up your list with a partner and explain why you have chosen your list. Put the group's choices in one main list and see if any common ideas emerge. Choose one idea and put together a ceremony to celebrate that special day.

Secret festivals

Even when Christian festivals have been totally forbidden, Christians have gone on celebrating their festivals in secret.

On Christmas Eve 1944, a German pastor celebrated Christmas in a Nazi prison with two other condemned prisoners and the prison governor. Of the four men present, one was sent to a concentration camp, another killed by the Gestapo, and the prison governor was removed from his post for being too humane. But the pastor could write of their service in the prison cells: 'We were prisoners – in the power of the Gestapo – in Berlin. But the peace of God enfolded us: it was real and present "like a Hand laid gently on us".'

● Why do you think Christians should want to go on celebrating their festivals in times of great difficulty and danger? In what ways might they be helped by these celebrations?

● With a partner imagine that people in this country were forbidden to celebrate Christmas and Easter Day. Do you think non-Christians would object? What would they miss? Why would Christians be especially upset?

Some Christians live with restrictions on what they can celebrate in public. Sometimes festivals aren't banned but life is made difficult for Christians in other ways. Sometimes this makes Christians stronger and more determined.

● Discuss the picture with a partner. Try to find out what country is shown and write a suitable caption.

Christian festivals

Christian festivals developed so that the Christian community would celebrate all the main stories and events in Jesus' life.

● Make a list of all the Christian festivals you know, and against each one write down the story or event in Jesus' life it celebrates.

People are sometimes surprised that most Christians regard one day every week as a festival. The Jews kept the seventh day of their week – the Sabbath – as their special day of rest and worship. The early Christians came to accept Sunday – the first day of the week, the day when Jesus rose from the dead – as their most important day. Every Sunday was a festival to remember the first Easter Day and to share the bread and wine. Eventually, when Christianity became the official religion of the Roman Empire, Sunday also became the day of rest.

ASSIGNMENTS

● Many people today feel that Sunday should be just like any other day. You might like to set up a class debate to put the arguments for and against. How do you think Christians would feel about this? Do some research to find out. Ask a number of people for their views. Collate the results and produce a report.

CHRISTMAS

● Christians have always used festivals to help their children learn more about their Christian faith. Make a collection (cards, Christmas paper, objects) showing the different stories, customs, symbols Christians could use to teach their children about the meaning of Christmas.

Most Christians find it easier to make and display the stories and symbols of Christmas than they do to explain their

A Christingle service

meaning and importance. Sometimes they put the two together in story-form. This is how a Christian minister explained the festival at a family service:

> 'Before Jesus came the people felt lost. They were in the dark. It was as if God had forgotten them. They were abandoned. Then God himself came into the world, like a light into the darkness, a saviour to their rescue. God became a human being in Jesus. Looking back in the writings of one of their prophets, they found just the words to describe what they felt. "The people that walked in darkness have seen a great light. They that dwelt in the land of the shadow of death, on them has the light shined."'

Christians describe God coming as a human person as the Incarnation (see page 21). Every year Christians prepare to celebrate again God's coming. They often use symbols of light to represent the idea of light coming into the darkness, and Christ as the 'light of the world'.

Christmas lights

Christians use lots of lights to celebrate Christmas. During the four weeks before Christmas when Christians are preparing for the coming (**Advent**) of Jesus and thinking seriously about what it means for their lives, many people have Advent wreaths. On each of the four Sundays before Christmas they light a new candle on the wreath or crown.

The Christmas festival lasts from Christmas Day to 6 January. Many churches have carol services illuminated by candles, and Christmas trees covered with coloured lights. For many the high point of Christmas is the Communion service or Mass, which ends early on Christmas Day morning. Everywhere there is a reminder about the light coming into the darkness.

Finally Christians celebrate **Epiphany** (on 6 January) – the story of the wise men, and the idea of Jesus as a gift not just for the Jews but for the whole world. Again light is used and in the picture you can see children with their own Christ-lights, or Christingles; an orange representing the world holds a candle to represent Christ as the Light of the World.

ASSIGNMENTS

● Look at the picture for a few moments. What do you think the idea of light and dark means to the small boy? Why do you think light is such an important symbol? Think about how you could express the idea of light coming into the darkness in visual ways. Create a symbol of Light and Dark through a picture, collage, or using other materials.

● Read the story of the wise men in Matthew 2:1–12. Every Christmas many Christians try to think how *they* should respond to the birth of Jesus: What does it mean to them? Using the story of the wise men write a talk explaining the meaning of Christmas for Christians.

KEY WORDS

Advent   Epiphany

EASTER

● A Christian magazine asked families to discuss: What is the most important event that has ever taken place in the history of the world? With a partner decide what you would say and what your answer shows about you. Decide what a Christian might say and the reasons they might give.

Holy Week

Because Easter is *the* event for most Christians, the weeks before Easter – **Lent** – are a time of special preparation. Many Christians still try to live simply at this time and give up some luxury. Often they meet together for Bible study or to talk about their beliefs. In the final days before Easter – Holy Week – Christians concentrate on the meaning of the last days of Jesus' life and his new life on Easter Day.

The Ceremony of Holy Fire at Easter

One Christian family, the Connors, share the Easter customs of their childhood. Mrs Connor teaches the children to make red eggs using onion skins, explaining how eggs symbolise new life, and red the colour of victory. Sometimes she makes hot-cross buns, getting the children to pipe the cross on top. The children especially enjoy making an Easter Garden. On Good Friday the 'tomb' is closed by a stone to show the death of Jesus. On Easter Day the tomb is opened and the 'garden' is decorated with spring flowers and Easter eggs.

● The Connor children enjoyed making an Easter Garden before they could understand all the symbolism of the spring flowers and eggs. Imagine you and your partner are making the Garden with them one year, when the seven-year-old says: 'Why do we put bright flowers and Easter eggs on the Garden when Jesus died?' How would you try to answer the question?

In Roman Catholic and some Anglican churches you will find fourteen Stations of the Cross – pictures or sculptures around the walls – showing important events in Jesus' final hours. Quietly, people look at each station, think about what happened and say a prayer about each event.

Easter Day

Some modern churches have a fifteenth station – the Resurrection – to show that Jesus' death wasn't the end but led to the victory of Easter Day. Roman Catholics have many ways of celebrating the victory. Mrs Connor describes what happens:

'On Good Friday the inside of the church is dark and bare with all the decorations covered or removed. The building is dark and dead. Then late on Easter Saturday there is a special Mass to wait for and celebrate the Resurrection. The Easter **Vigil** is so special to me. Outside the church a fire is lit and then the priest carries the large **paschal** candle bearing the new light inside and the light is spread all through the congregation. In the darkness the light symbolises the new life of Christ on Easter morning, just as the women went to the tomb in the story and found the stone rolled away and the message "He is risen." After that, all the gold and white vestments, the flowers and music seem so right.'

ASSIGNMENTS

● During Holy Week the Connors, like millions of Christians, spend more time in church than at any other point in the year. They remember the things that happened to Jesus in Jerusalem, and reflect on why they are still important. Look at three:
a) Palm Sunday (Mark 11:1–11)
b) Maundy Thursday (Mark 14:12–52)
c) Good Friday (Mark 15:1–47)
Use the books listed on page 64 to find out what Christians do on each of these days to remember what happened to Jesus. Describe what happens in your own words.

KEY WORDS

Lent   vigil   paschal

PENTECOST

People are always looking for power, strength, energy. The cartoon character Popeye used to get his from eating spinach. Advertisers try to tell people they'll get power from drinking a particular fizzy drink or even milk.

● Find some other examples of how people try to symbolise the idea of great power and energy.

A gift of power

In the Acts of the Apostles chapters 1 and 2, you can see how the early Christians tried to describe the gift of power and energy they received. Jesus had overcome death and shared his new life with his disciples. Although he left them forty days after Easter (Ascension Day), ten days later at the Feast of **Pentecost** they were meeting in Jerusalem, trying to decide what to do and waiting for the power and strength he had promised them. Here is a modern writer describing what happened. You can compare his version with that in Acts 2:1–4:

The disciples were back in Jerusalem. Jesus had left them. They knew they would never see him again. But he was not dead; his spirit was still there. If only they could feel it. They sat and looked at one another. And then it

happened. The room was dull and quiet. The only light came from the tiny windows; the only sound was the crowd in the street outside. Suddenly it was all changed. There seemed to be a rumbling sound and a movement in the air. It felt as if a strong wind were beating through the house. The disciples looked up. Across the room they gazed at one another. They glowed. There was no other word for it. It was as if they were on fire. A minute ago they had been gloomy. Now each of them suddenly felt more alive than he had ever felt before. They started to talk and shout. Most of the words didn't seem to make any sense but it didn't matter.

● Look at the picture. In what ways does this symbolise the idea of power and energy? Do you think it is a good picture to illustrate Pentecost?

Ascension and Pentecost

On **Ascension** Day the paschal candle
is lit for the last time. At Pentecost there
are special readings, hymns and red
decorations to celebrate the gift of the
Spirit. Christians sometimes call Pentecost
'the birthday of the Church'. A week later,
on Trinity Sunday, Christians celebrate
their belief that God is dynamic, active,
living – he is Father, Son and Holy Spirit.

   Some Christians believe that the gift of
the Spirit is shown by special signs –
'speaking in tongues', healing and
prophecy. These are the same gifts or
'charisma' Christians received in the early
Church, and so Christians who think like
this, inside and outside the major
Churches, are called **Charismatics**.
Sometimes they are also called
Pentecostalists, after the gift of the Spirit at
Pentecost.

ASSIGNMENTS

● If you had to draw or choose a picture to represent the
power of Pentecost, what would you want it to show? Draw
your picture or write a piece explaining what you would
look for.

● Write a diary entry or conversation as if you had been one
of the disciples sitting in the Upper Room in Jerusalem at
the Feast of Pentecost. Imagine you were trying to answer
the questions 'What happened? What did you feel? How are
you different?' If you decide on a conversation you could
act it out with a partner for the rest of the group.

● The Pentecostalist or Charismatic Churches are some of the
fastest growing in Great Britain today. Use the books on
page 64 to find out about their main ideas. See if you can
discover any local groups to visit or write about.

KEY WORDS

Pentecost   Ascension   Charismatic

THE CHRISTIAN YEAR

● With a partner, think about the shape of your year. Does it begin in January, or in September with the school year, or with a religious festival? What are the high points of your year? Now using a Christian calendar, draw a graph showing the shape of the Christian year.

'A year that shapes my life'

For some Christians, the Christian year not only has a particular pattern but it gives their own lives a shape and purpose as well. Here one Christian describes her year:

'I was brought up a Roman Catholic and so going to Mass on festival days was part of my childhood. The Church's year somehow seemed to fit in with mine. My birthday was in November so it seemed quite right to start the year with Advent and all the preparations for Christmas. Then there was the long period of Lent so we got used to going without sweets and cake. Even in Lent there were special days. We always had pancakes on Shrove Tuesday and went to be ashed on Ash Wednesday. I remember meeting a school friend in the street as we came out with the mark of the ashes on our foreheads. She gave me a funny look. Then our church was dedicated to St Patrick so we had a great Patronal Festival with a parish party afterwards. We used to look forward to March 17th with great excitement.

I think my friends at school thought it was odd we spent so much time in church. But my mother was especially devoted to the Blessed Virgin Mary and used to go to Mass on all her special days. It never occurred to me not to go with her though my father didn't come very often. I know some Christians don't approve of any of this but it did keep God in the centre of my life and I don't regret it at all. Young people today seem so aimless while my life always had a shape.'

● Someone who knows very little about Christianity might find this passage difficult to understand. What parts would they find especially difficult? Make a list with a partner and then decide how you would explain each one.

Not all Christian groups approve of or keep the same festivals or have their church dedicated to a special saint. Most Anglican and Roman Catholic churches in England are dedicated to a saint and have a special Patronal Festival on the day set aside in the church's calendar for that saint.

ASSIGNMENTS

What can you see in the picture to suggest what point in the Christian year this might be? What clues does the picture provide? Imagine you are present and reporting the event for a newspaper. Write or tape a short report indicating the time in the Christian year and explaining the event using the clues the picture gives.

Make a list of the different churches in your district. Find out what they are called and what is their special or patronal day and how they celebrate it.

If you had to name a new Christian church, which saint or living Christian would you choose and why? Write a short piece explaining your choice. Produce a brief ceremony of dedication for the new church, using symbols, words, a song or hymn and ritual.

VALUES

LOVE IN ACTION

The price of love

⬤ Look carefully at the picture. Describe what you see. What qualities would be required of a person who wanted to help this man?

Now read this case study:

A group of local Christians have got together to try and help the many homeless men and women, like the man in the picture, who sleep rough in the city

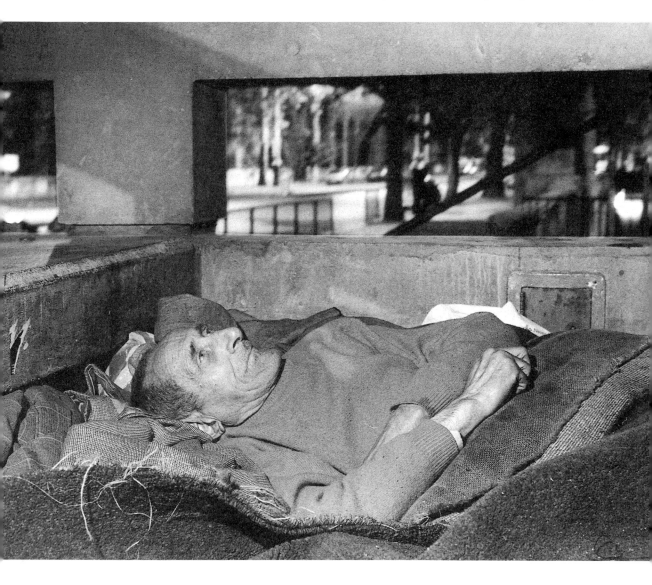

streets. They produce evidence that many of these people have no homes to go to, and no families to support them. You give some money and support the campaign to try to find housing for them. Then you learn that a wealthy property owner has been so moved by their difficulties that he has made a house in your road available for bed-sits to house six of the most desperate cases. Some of your friends and neighbours are up in arms about this – arguing that the hostel will reduce the value of the neighbouring houses, bring undesirables into the road, and be a risk to local children. They ask you what you think and invite you to go to a local protest meeting.

● What would you do? You care for the homeless people, but you also care for your friends and neighbours. What would you say at the protest meeting? Share your ideas with a partner.

The example of Jesus

Christians aren't the only ones to care about other people. But the first Christians believed Jesus had given them special instructions about caring and loving. In John's Gospel Jesus says:

'I give you a new commandment: love one another; as I have loved you, so you are to love one another.'

[John 13:34]

Paul tried to explain what Christian love involved. He wrote to the people of Corinth:

⁴Love is patient, love is kind. It does not envy, it does not boast, it is not proud. ⁵It is not rude, it is not self-seeking, it is not easily angered, it keeps no record of wrongs. ⁶Love does not delight in evil but rejoices with the truth. ⁷It always protects, always trusts, always hopes, always perseveres.

⁸Love never fails.

[1 Corinthians 13:4–8]

Some Christians think his description also describes Jesus. Try reading the passage 'Jesus is patient, Jesus is kind. Jesus does not envy . . .'.

ASSIGNMENTS

● Look again at the case study. In groups imagine you are each one of the different people involved in the situation:
a) one of the people with no home
b) one of those living near the proposed hostel
c) one of the local Christian group.
Discuss first how the Christian attitude might be different or distinctive, then act out the viewpoint you think each of these would take. Afterwards write down the speech you think the Christian might give at the protest meeting.

● Some people say love is soft and easy. Find and describe the work of a Christian and/or Christian organisation to show whether this is an accurate description. (Here are a few ideas to get you started: Cicely Saunders and the hospice movement; Leonard Cheshire and the Cheshire Homes; Sybil Phoenix and community relations.)

LOVE YOUR ENEMIES

● Spend a few minutes thinking about any time you have been hurt by what someone has said or done to you. Can you remember how deeply you felt? What did you want to say back to the person concerned? Were you ever able to forgive the person who mistreated you? How would you feel about someone who attempted to hurt you very seriously?

People often suffer the most appalling mistreatment during the stress and horror of war. It can also present those involved with very difficult decisions. In this account from the Second World War some English officers, recently set free from a Japanese prisoner-of-war camp, find themselves next to a trainload of wounded Japanese soldiers. For years they had been starved and tortured by the Japanese soldiers who had been their prison guards.

Farther on we were shunted on to a siding for a lengthy stay. We found ourselves on the same track with several carloads of Japanese wounded. They were on their own and without medical care. No longer fit for action, they had been packed into railway trucks which were being returned to Bangkok. Whenever one of them died en route he was thrown off into the jungle. They were in a shocking state. Their uniforms were encrusted with mud, blood and excrement. Their wounds, sorely inflamed and full of pus, crawled with

maggots ... Without a word most of the officers in my section unbuckled their packs, took out most of their rations and a rag or two, and with water canteens in their hands went over to the Japanese train to help them. Our guards tried to prevent us, bawling, 'No goodka! No goodka!' But we ignored them and knelt by the side of the enemy to give them food and water, to clean and bind their wounds, to smile and say a kind word. Grateful cries of 'Agratto!' (thank you) followed when we left. An allied officer from another section of the train had been taking it all in. 'What bloody fools you all are!', he said to me. 'Don't you realise those are the enemy?'

● Imagine yourself with the prisoners of war when the Japanese wounded came alongside. What would you have done? Who do you think was right – the officers who helped or the allied officer who called them 'bloody fools' for assisting the enemy?

The example of Jesus

Christians try to follow the teaching of Jesus found in Matthew's Gospel.

● Read Matthew 5:43–8 and try to explain what he is saying in one sentence.

Even more powerful for Christians than Jesus' teaching is the example of love and forgiveness he gave them with his death. Luke's Gospel describes how Jesus was taken to a place outside the city of Jerusalem and crucified. The Gospel reports (23:34):

> Jesus said, 'Father, forgive them, they do not know what they are doing.'

Christians believe that if they follow Jesus they must be prepared to forgive in the same way.

ASSIGNMENTS

● Christians still try to follow Jesus' example today. Read the newspaper article and then write a brief account in your own words. Include in your comments why most people were impressed by Mr Wilson's words; why some people were surprised by what he said; and why others were angry at them. Then write briefly about your own reaction.

Enniskillen, November 1987

I FORGIVE her killers. . . . The words were spoken today by the 60-year-old father of his 20-year-old daughter who was murdered in the Enniskillen massacre.

"I am sorry for them, but I bear them no ill-will," said Gordon Wilson. "I prayed for them last night."

Mr Wilson and daughter Marie were buried under 6ft of stone and rubble when the bomb went off.

They held hands and tried to comfort each other until help came.

Four times Mr Wilson asked Marie if she was Okay. Each time she replied she was all right.

"I asked her the fifth time and she said: 'Daddy, I love you very much.' Those were her last words," said Mr Wilson.

He recalled that five minutes after the explosion, rescuers were pulling him out of the rubble. He told them: "Boys, I'm all right. But for God's sake my daughter is lying right beside me and I don't think she's too well. She's dead."

Actually Marie underwent five hours of surgery for brain damage, a crushed pelvis and severe internal bleeding. Doctors said she then died.

"For the last 40 years I've gone to the Enniskillen ceremony," he said. " Marie said she'd like to come. Her mum couldn't because she plays organ at church and said she'd have to be there."

Of the killer blast, he said: " It wasn't loud. I was pushed forward on my face and the rubble of the wall and the railings fell on top of us and I thought I was not badly hurt. . . I then felt

somebody holding my hand quite firmly. It was Marie and she said ' Are you all right, Daddy.' I said ' Yes,' "

Mr Wilson said that in between holding hands Marie was shouting an dscreaming with what I took to be pain. I couldn't understand why she was saying she was all right, but screaming.

Mr Wilson went on: 'I haven't thought about the wider, political implications. All I know is that we have lost a gorgeous girl.

"Someone said this morning that this could be a turning point, let's pray that it is. We have a heartbroken home; we have lost a lovely girl.

"I am helped by the fact that lots of people are praying for us

"I am certain that God will give me, my wife and my family the grace to come through this.

"I believe this is part of a bigger plan. I don't understand it but if I didn't believe it I would commit suicide."

FAITH UNDER FIRE

• Wedding couples often send a present list to their families and friends with gifts they would like as presents. If you could give a newly married couple three qualities (e.g. patience, sense of humour, etc.) rather than a coffee-maker or toaster, what three qualities do you think would be most useful in their lives together? Spend a few minutes thinking about your choice and be ready to explain your ideas to a friend or a group.

Christian families face all the same sort of problems any family does. It is not always easy to see from the outside what difference the Christian commitment of the parents or the children makes. Read this comment from a single parent who was left to bring up two children by herself.

'At first when my husband walked out on me, I was as bitter as anyone would be in the same situation. I felt so hurt and betrayed. I felt so inadequate. I was certain the people at church would think I'd failed, and want to have nothing to do with us any more. A few were like that but most couldn't have been kinder – they were a life-line until I got back on my feet again, listening to me going over and over everything so many times, looking after the children when I needed to have a few hours' break, providing practical help with leaking pipes and worn-out cars.

It took quite a few months but gradually I began to see that God hadn't abandoned me like I first thought. He'd been working through the love and practical care of friends. A close friend helped me to understand that if I had been betrayed then that didn't mean I couldn't trust anyone. If I had failed, then God could help me to make a fresh start, could help me to start understanding my husband even if I couldn't yet forgive him, could let me see the possibility of a new life ahead. That helped me to help the children. They needed me to be strong because they were even more confused and frightened than I was. I think because I kept my faith that God wouldn't totally abandon us, that kept their confidence going as well. I wouldn't wish this on anyone but you really find out what means most to you in this sort of situation.'

• Why might a Christian in this situation feel God had let them down? What other sort of events could put a Christian's faith to the test? In what different ways did the woman in the quotation find her Christian faith helped her?

ASSIGNMENTS

• Christians are involved in many organisations which try to help individuals and families in trouble. Some are specifically Christian; others have no special religious connection. Find out about the work of two of the following, one Christian and one non-religious: The Children's Society, the Simon Community or The Mothers' Union (Christian), Samaritans or Relate/Marriage Guidance (non-religious). Describe any important differences and similarities you find between the Christian and non-religious organisations you have studied.

• Why do you think a Christian might want to help with the work of any of these organisations? Produce a newspaper/magazine article with appropriate picture and headings from either a real or imaginary interview with a Christian volunteer.

LIFE AS A JOURNEY

● With a partner talk about the different ways you could illustrate your life as a journey. What pictures or main events would you include in your description of the journey so far? If you could map the journey 10, 20 or 30 years on, what events, successes or goals would you like to include?

Pilgrimages

Often Christians use real journeys to help them think about their lives and to get closer to God. Many believe that places where Jesus or some outstanding Christians (**saints**) lived are holy. By travelling to Jerusalem or Rome pilgrims feel they are travelling closer to God. Together with other pilgrims they visit the famous sites, attend services and pray, sometimes seeking forgiveness for things they have done wrong. Often the pilgrim is looking for some special assistance from God – healing for some physical or mental illness, a solution to a problem, help with an important decision. This is one person's experience:

I went to Jerusalem and the Holy Land as a tourist because a Christian friend wanted company. At first I was so disappointed by how crowded everywhere was: Bethlehem, Nazareth, even Jerusalem. And so many people wanting to sell cheap souvenirs. Nothing seemed real at all – Jesus

seemed a thousand miles away; until we got to Galilee. And there by the lake just as the sun came up we had a Communion service and it suddenly all came alive for me. The leader read the story of Jesus having breakfast with his disciples after the Resurrection – and telling Peter 'Follow me'. And I knew – after all the years of pretending – that those words were meant for me as well, just as if Jesus was looking back to where I sat and saying 'Follow me'. The leader said I went as a tourist and came back a pilgrim. Nothing has ever had the same effect on me before or since.

The writer of this passage came back home and found her values and goals completely changed. Some of the things she once thought important now seemed unimportant; other small things now seemed to matter a great deal.

● If someone takes Christianity really seriously, what would you expect them to think were the most important things in their life? In what ways do you think this could make them difficult or easy to live with?

ASSIGNMENTS

● Look quietly at the picture of the place which meant so much to the writer. Is there any place where you would want to go to think about the purpose and meaning of your life because it has a special importance to you? Write a piece of poetry or prose to describe your place and why it is important to you.

● Jerusalem   Assisi (Italy)   Rome
Walsingham (England)   Lourdes (France)   Taizé (France)
Find out why modern-day pilgrims go to any *one* of the
places listed above, how they get there and what special
things they do or see on their pilgrimage. What special
reasons might they have for choosing their destination?

● When you have done your research:
Either write a letter home as if you were a pilgrim,
describing why you went, what you saw and what you felt
on your pilgrimage,
or write a three- to five-minute account for radio, describing
the experience of modern-day pilgrimage, and record your
script on tape.

KEY WORDS

saint

The Sea of Galilee

Glossary

Advent 'Coming' – season of preparation for celebration of Jesus' coming at Christmas

Anglican World-wide fellowship of Christians centred on Canterbury (e.g. Church of England, Church in Wales)

Ascension Belief that Jesus was taken up to heaven celebrated 40 days after Easter

Atonement Belief that through Jesus' death human beings are restored to their relationship with God

baptism Special words and actions which admit people to the Christian Church

Baptist Church founded in the 17th century. They believe only adults should be baptised

Bible From a word meaning 'books'. The Old Testament describes the life of the Jews up to the time of Jesus. The New Testament is about Jesus and the first Christians

Charismatic Christian who lays special emphasis on gifts of the Spirit

Communion Sharing of bread and wine that obeys Jesus' command at the Last Supper

confirmation Ceremony in which some Christians take on their baptism promises for themselves, and the gift of the Spirit is renewed

Creator Title for God following Christian and Jewish belief that the world was brought into being by God

creed Statement of Christian beliefs; e.g. the Apostles' Creed and the Nicene Creed

crucifix Cross with a figure of Jesus crucified

Epiphany 'Appearance' – festival on January 6, based on the story of the wise men, celebrating Jesus as a gift to all people

Eucharist Another word for sharing the bread and wine, stressing idea of 'thanksgiving'

Gospel 'Good news' – the preaching of Jesus and the accounts of his life and meaning by Matthew, Mark, Luke and John

icon Painting of Jesus or one of the saints used in the Orthodox Church to help worshippers in their prayers

Incarnation Belief that God came into human life as Jesus

Lent Period of preparation for Easter lasting 40 days from Ash Wednesday to Easter Saturday (excluding Sundays)

liturgy Term used to describe words and actions in services, especially Communion in the Orthodox Churches

Mass Name for sharing of bread and wine in Roman Catholic Church

Methodist Church founded through the work of John Wesley in the 18th century

Orthodox Eastern Churches going back to the first churches founded by the Apostles

paschal Refers to Jewish Passover; since Jesus died at Passover time it also describes things to do with Easter

Pentecost Festival 50 days after Easter which celebrates the gift of God's Holy Spirit to the first Christians

priest Person in the Roman Catholic and Anglican Churches ordained by a bishop, with the authority to celebrate the Communion. Protestant Churches often have ministers or pastors instead

Protestant Term to describe most Christians who do not belong to Roman Catholic or Orthodox Churches, dating from 16th-century Reformation (e.g. Baptists)

Quakers Popular name for those who belong to the Society of Friends, founded in the 17th century

Resurrection Belief that after his death on Good Friday Jesus rose to new life on Easter Day

Roman Catholic Church that accepts the authority of the Pope as the successor to St Peter (Matthew 16:18–19)

rosary Set of prayers in the Roman Catholic Church; also a string of 165 beads to help worshippers say these prayers

sacrament Action and symbol that conveys God's blessing

saint Title used in the New Testament for all Christians, but normally kept for Christians who have shown outstanding commitment to God

vigil A time of watching and prayer before a special occasion, e.g. Easter Vigil

Index

Further reading

The Alternative Service Book. Hodder & Stoughton, 1980 (*Church of England*)

The Methodist Service Book. Methodist Publishing House, 1975

The Sunday Missal. Collins, 1975 (*Roman Catholic*)

Alves, C. *et al. The Question of Jesus*, Church House Publishing, 1987

Bentley, J. and A. Bentley. *Contemporary Issues: A Christian View*, Longman, 1989

Brine, A. *Worship: An Exploration*, Macmillan, 1987

Brown, A. *Christian Communities* (Chichester Project), Lutterworth, 1982

—— *The Christian World*, Macdonald, 1984

Brown, A., J. Rankin and A. Wood. *Religions*, Longman, 1988

Cross, V. *Jesus*, Holt, Rinehart & Winston, 1984

Cross, V. and P. Taylor. *Christian Worship*, Holt, Rinehart & Winston, 1985

Curtis, P. *Exploring the Bible* (Chichester Project), Lutterworth, 1984

—— *The Christians' Book* (Chichester Project), Lutterworth, 1984

Erricker, C. *Christian Ethics* (Chichester Project), Lutterworth, 1984

Gower, R. *Frontiers*, Lion, 1983

Harrison, S. and D. Shepherd. *A Christian Family in Britain*, RMEP, 1985

Naylor, D. and A. Smith. *Jesus: An Enquiry*, Macmillan, 1985

Perkins, J. and A. Brown. *Dictionaries of World Religions: Christianity*, Batsford, 1988

Priestley, J. (ed.) *The Living Festivals Series*, RMEP

Rankin, J. *Christian Worship* (Chichester Project), Lutterworth, 1982

—— *The Eucharist* (Chichester Project), Lutterworth, 1985

Read, G. *et al. Christians* Book 3 (Westhill Project), Mary Glasgow, 1987

—— *Christians* Book 4 (Westhill Project), Mary Glasgow, 1987

Shannon, T. *Christmas and Easter* (Chichester Project), Lutterworth, 1984

—— *Jesus* (Chichester Project), Lutterworth, 1982

Thompson, J. and M. Thompson. *The Many Paths of Christianity*, Edward Arnold, 1988

LONGMAN GROUP UK LIMITED
Longman House, Burnt Mill, Harlow,
Essex CM20 2JE, England
and Associated Companies throughout the world.

© Longman Group UK Limited 1991
All rights reserved. No part of this publication may be reproduced, stored
in a retrieval system, or transmitted in any form or by any means,
electronic, mechanical, photocopying, recording, or otherwise without
either the prior written permission of the Publishers or a licence
permitting restricted copying issued by the Copyright Licensing Agency Ltd,
33–34 Alfred Place, London WC1E 7DP.

First published 1991
ISBN 0 582 02970 8

Set in 11/14 Garamond
Produced by Longman Group (FE) Ltd
Printed in Hong Kong